On Love

Poems From The Heart

By

Carol Melber

On Love

On Love

Author of:

The Rolling Moon

Jumping Jellybeans

Independent Publisher November, 2016

Manufactured in the United States of America

ISBN: 0-9983486-0-0
ISBN-13: 978-0-9983486-0-5

DEDICATION

This book is for everyone who has experienced love
and all the rest who are destined to do so.

Contents

Acknowledgments

These
original poems
were inspired by
real relationships,
some fleeting,
others
not.
I
treasure
each equally
as a precious gift
that brought me closer
to my present understanding
of the beauty, pain, joy and wonder
that is
love.

Lovers Rejoice

So what be a lover?

Surely not merely

one filled with hot lust

seeking only

the taking.

Embraces short-lived,

while long-awaiting true wonders,

are not worthy a name

associated with

the true passion

of love.

For passion comes

from the core of the heart

and the heart rules

love

On Love

on all levels.

Lovers rejoice!

In open-aired gladless.

For to feed a trusting love

is to nourish a soul.

Admire the lovers!

They are the core

of human existence

and together

as one

they

will

rule

all

eternity.

Rejection

Relationships are stages

of learning truths,

filled with

revelations

that bond people together

and sometimes

tear them apart.

First impression images

are mostly

what you alone can see.

what you alone

choose to see

while you continue searching

for your idea

of perfection

On Love

in

someone else.

Unfair!

The burdened-cross

for someone else to bear,

someone who

you thought you would love,

could love,

one day,

maybe even

as soon as

tomorrow.

Someone who

you thought would

love you

stronger than

anyone had ever

before.

On Love

Someone who

you see

look the other way

before

you had even one

sweet moment

to remember.

So who's to blame then,

for all this illusion?

How do you sort it out?

Do you revisit your heart's secrets

in hopes

of finding

that it was all

just

a simple mistake?

It was all

just

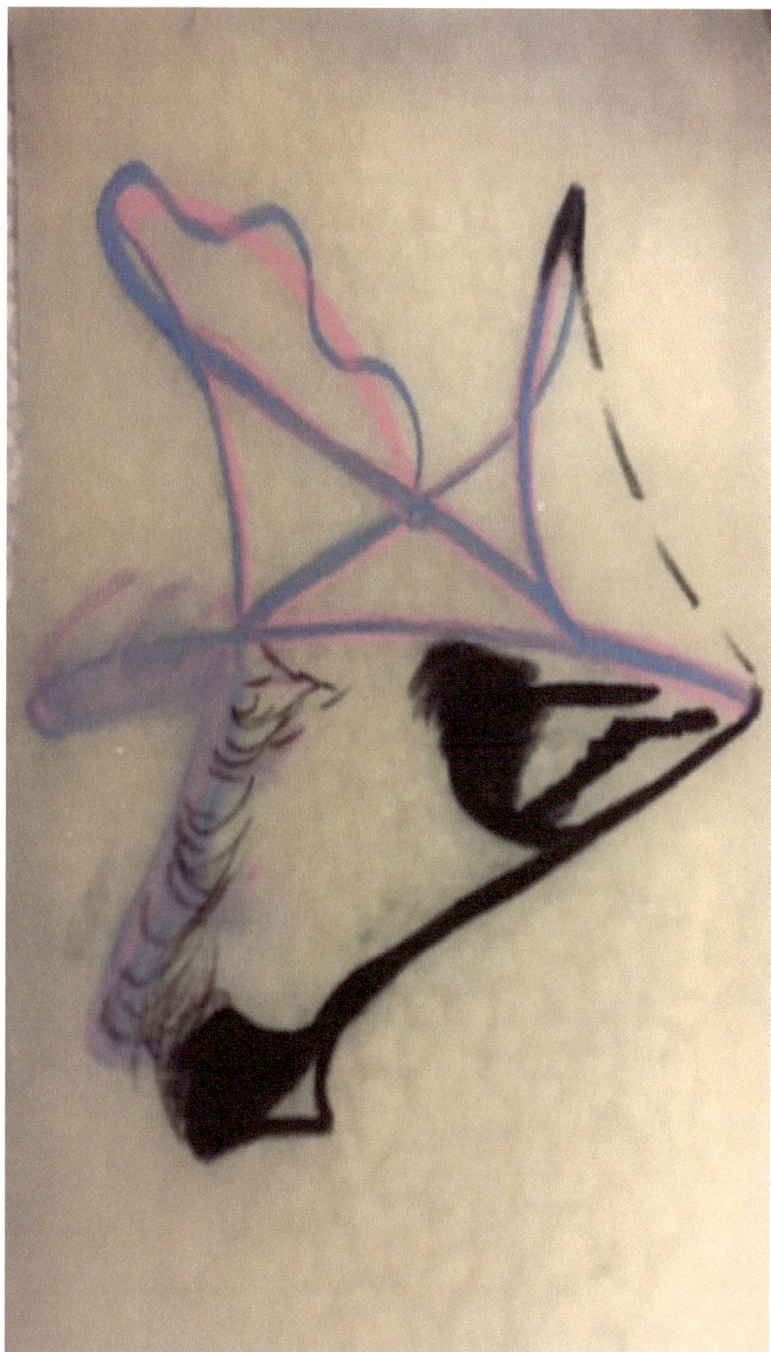

On Love

a misunderstanding or

some emotional embellishment or

fantasy on your part?

Do you sift through the desires

kept hidden in the depths

of your soul and try to uncover

another path, the right path

you were surely

meant to follow?

Or

do you avoid

locating the culprit,

and instead play

a little game

of hide and seek

for awhile

choosing denial

for temporary comfort?

On Love

Eventually,

inevitably,

you will be ready

to move forward.

Then you can seek

another remedy

to quash the awkward feelings

of uncertainty

and insecurity

that may haunt your thoughts

sometimes with persistence,

like a nagging realization

at the start of a day

that follows after

receiving bad news.

That day,

seeps into the next day

with the same

On Love

lingering

and hurtful memory.

Eventually you compromise,

your find a way to move forward

with no regrets,

no sorrow,

no

bitterness.

You choose

to be brave

and face the truth.

You choose

to turn a stinging moment

of realizing rejection

into a better truth,

an epiphany

that brings

some peace of mind.

On Love

Then perchance

it brings

a touch of happiness

when you reason

that after all

you are a lucky one

who felt love's power

and wonder.

Now you know

that the rewards

of experience

will remain with you

as you journey on

in your life

wiser now

and more ready

for the next time.

Yearning

I dreamed you said to me "I love you."

then we sealed my echo

with the kind of kiss

reserved by some,

and not for public view.

I wanted to tell you,

but instead I waited,

in silence,

until the desire left me,

just like a puff of smoke

swirling the emotion

of regret

around in my head.

Later,

I saw those same words

On Love

written

on a billboard

ahead and on the right side

of the highway

we traveled every day.

I hadn't really noticed

the sign before that moment,

even though I must have seen it

a dozen times before.

As we drove closer,

close enough to see

the happiness

advertised by the would be lovers

posing for that photograph,

I wanted to draw your attention

to them

as if to say,

"Hey, look!"

On Love

"That could be us!"

but instead

I hesitated and

we passed by

in uninterrupted silence.

Now,

it all seems

like someone else's life.

Now,

you are absent

from my dreams.

Now,

We no longer drive

anywhere

together.

Now,

I feel that

On Love

the door is closing

and I'm afraid

my love for you

may not be

powerful enough

to stop it.

I want to cry out!

I want you for my friend!

I want you for my lover!

I want you

to say to me

"I love you."

On Love

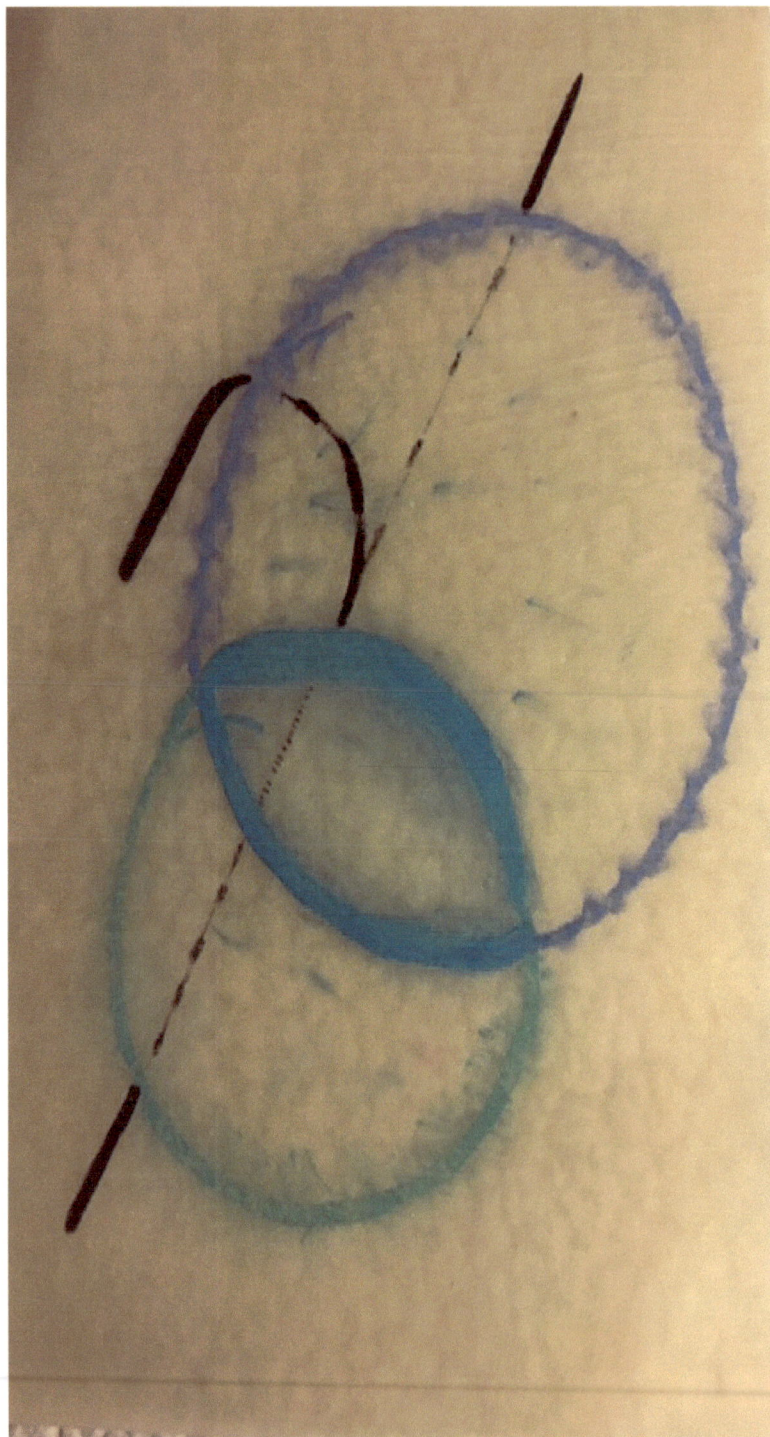

Your Eyes

Today,

for the first time,

I saw your eyes up close.

I saw them close enough

to see fire mixed with color.

Yours?

Or mine reflected?

I was startled, pleasantly.

I was also surprised

I had not noticed before.

I think I could love you.

Maybe

Something

about you

attracts my attention.

Something

about the possibility

of us

excites me.

Somehow

I think I know

that perhaps

you may have thought this too.

Maybe,

tomorrow

nothing will change.

Maybe

On Love

everything will

be just slightly different.

Even if

you cannot

or will not

or do not

want

this,

I am quite certain

now at least

one thing will remain the same.

Even if

I can never have you

I will not lose my desire

for you

for us

for sometime.

Rebound

When we met

you were allergic

to things like love and commitment.

Each time those subjects arose

you broke out

in a rash of excuses

to hide the pain.

I knew

that after therapy,

and mostly time,

you would recover

to become yourself

as you once were,

when you were free

and alive with emotions

On Love

even you

could not fully control.

You would recover stronger,

and ready to open your heart.

I would have waited then.

You were too restless and moved on.

It was so hard to see you go.

Months later,

my heart pounded with excitement

when I saw your face.

Then I saw her,

standing close,

with her arm linked through yours.

You turned to look at her

and I could see

tenderness and love in your gaze.

On Love

I wanted to look away

but I had to see.

I had to see that part of you

that part that eluded me,

eluded us.

Now,

I am happy for you,

I am happy that you can feel

again.

I am only sorry

I was not the one

to administer the anecdote.

I Never Met Her

I never met her.

I only knew her

through your subtle displays

of anger,

and disappointment,

and mostly

through your spoken words

of mistrust

and a slight distain

for the female gender,

generally.

I ignored

the fact that you must have known

even if you tried not to,

I was a member

of her gentler kind.

Still,

I knew I didn't like her

because she hurt you hard.

More than this though,

I didn't like her

because

she left you

with a wound

deeper

than

the promise of

a relationship with me

could begin to heal.

I Was So Sure

You may not have known,

while I thought

it was so obvious.

You were my goal.

I was so sure,

that you could read

the smile

in my eyes

each time you commented

on my independence.

I was so sure

I knew you well enough.

I even let you go

to that place

far away from me

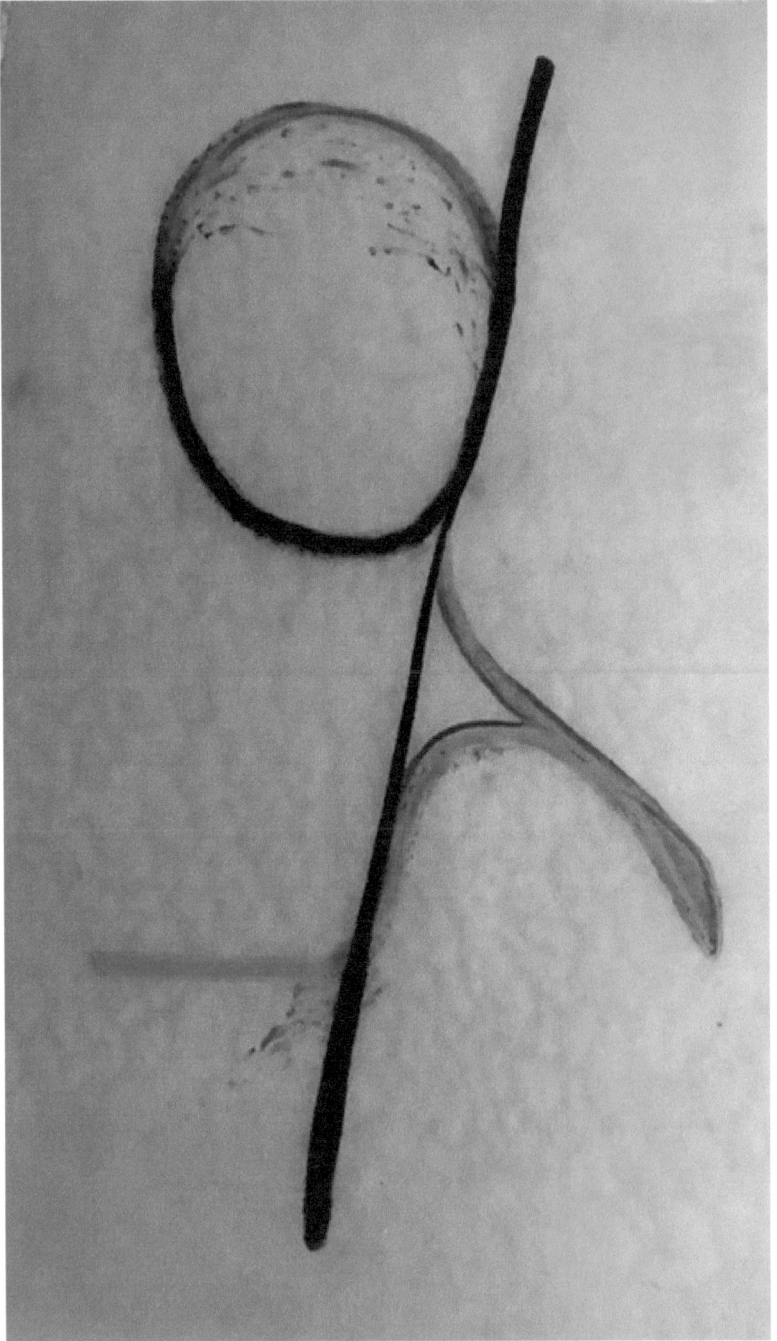

On Love

from us.

I did not even try to follow

because I was so sure

that I knew you.

We could not have been better

at being friends.

If only

we had not been lovers too.

I was so sure,

you knew I was waiting.

I was so sure,

you were waiting too.

Now,

I just feel foolish.

I could not read your heart.

What I will never know,

or understand,

On Love

or care to,

is why

you chose to be so damn polite

all the way

to the end

of the relationship

you never knew

we had.

Perfect Day

If you told me

that I could fly

in a time machine.

I would not want to see

you in a yesterday.

I would not want to be

in a tomorrow

somewhere.

I would just want

to spend a day

like this one, now

with you.

With You

With you

I will seek knowledge

of life's sea

We are gatherers
taking refuge in
our treasures,
sentimental only
with our pride.

For you

I will share time

We count our blessings
like keeping score,
using measurements
still unknown.

To you

I will give myself
gladly accepting
some of you in return.

When We Part

When we part,

I am not going to promise

anything.

I will not say that I will see you

again.

If you need

someone like me,

look away.

I will not lie

and say I will stay for you.

I will not.

All you will have

is our time

together.

now.

On Love

So lock it away

and use it

as you will,

as you may need to

someday.

That is all it is meant to be.

Don't expect any more

from me

when I am gone,

when we part.

If Ever

If ever

there comes a time

when a love of mine

shows all the signs of leaving,

I promise

myself

this much at least:

I promise I will ask

why

and once I am satisfied

with the answer,

I will ask myself

do I still care?

If my answer is no

I will say goodbye.

On Love

If my answer is yes

I promise myself

I will stay my emotions

and ask my love

to please

not go.

Trust

When I can confide

everything uncertain

and don't wish that I had not

after.

When I can let go

myself

to let you take charge

of my life

for a day,

or even a moment

then easily forget

I had

after.

When I can fall asleep

near you

anytime

On Love

in any place

and find simple comfort

knowing you

are within a short reach

to touch

to love

to hold

after.

Any of these

should tell you

I trust you.

Fickle

Beginnings and endings

streams full of enthusiasm

and loss

along a somewhat reckless path

to a complete education.

Complete only in that

the never-ending yearn

will forever render it

incomplete.

See how

the same accomplishment

that at first fulfills a dark void

will just as surely

carry loneliness,

a mock companion,

like the scent of snow in the air

On Love

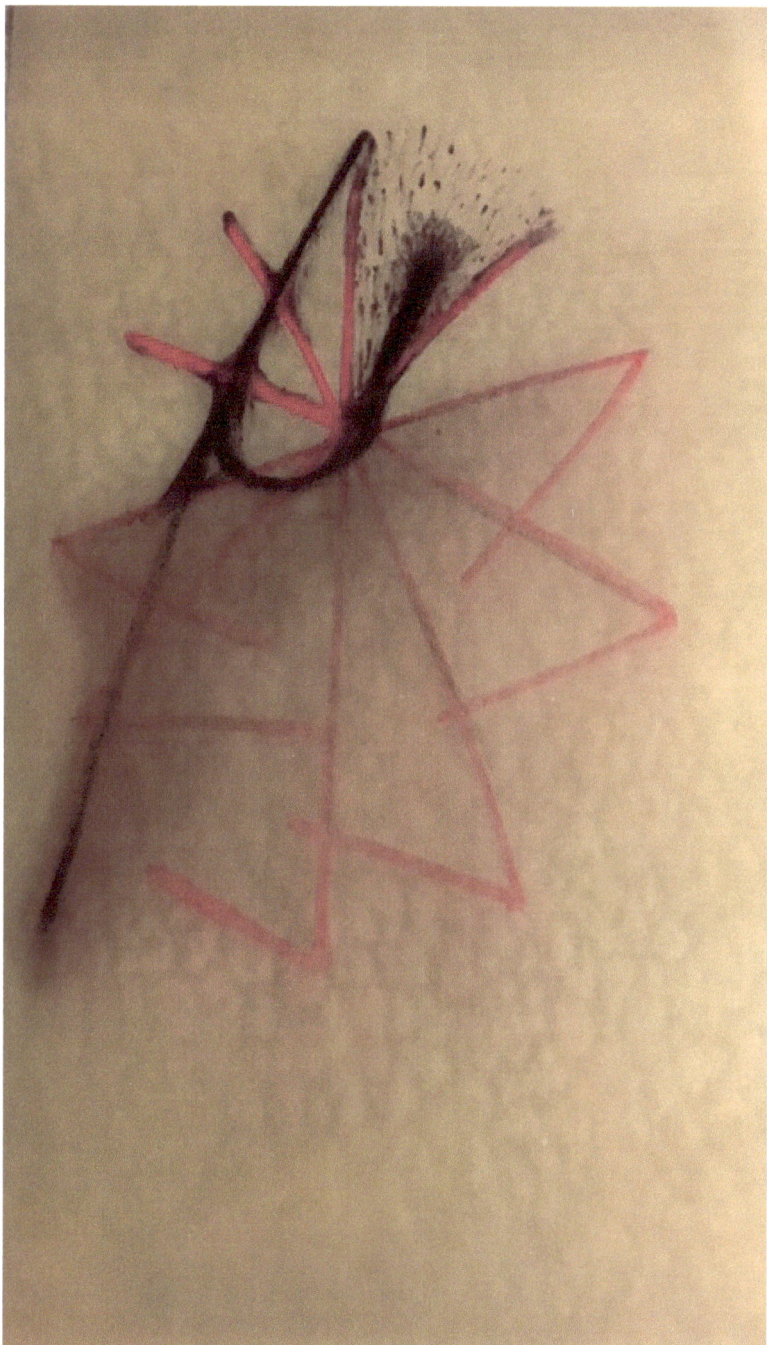

On Love

under a darkening sky

in early spring

after daffodils are in bloom.

For some men I think

women are accomplishments,

steps to climb

to the next landing,

where awaits them

only

a disillusioned state of mind.

The cycle continues,

yearning continues

for another challenge,

another possibility,

another accomplishment.

Buying Time

Have you noticed

there are certain people

who need presents

before

they can be a friend?

I suppose

if the gift was good enough

their friendship

would last

that much longer.

Maybe those people

have too many clocks

on their walls

or just one

big enough

to measure

49

On Love

their hearts by.

I am so glad

we never needed presents

or clocks

to measure

or compare

our friendship.

Midnight Questions

Midnight questions spark fires.

One to remember,

none to decide.

Yes,

you are

sought clearly.

The illuminated passages

in our minds

hold images

of a past rewritten and

a hopeful future.

We stay

more or less,

in the present,

in between

the difference we could have made

and the second chance

we hope to gain.

Still,

you are sought dearly.

The words,

spoken in symbols.

leave only blank paper behind.

You stand as alone

among the many others

who

are only wanting one brief embrace.

Then,

as a fleeting shadow

you will be gone,

running

somewhere, nowhere,

just

On Love

gone.

Running with a truth, your truth

disguised in daylight as a purpose.

I am left

holding on to the hopes

that thrive in darkness.

I am left

still pushing back

thoughts of indecision.

I am left

wondering

was it all just an illusion?

The answer will not come,

Leaving me with just fuzzy memories

of a fading question

until

it doesn't matter

anymore.

Yule Tidings

It is that time of year.

Decorations up and

music everywhere

sending me

on a memory tour.

I wonder what you think

when you see a house all lit up,

all inviting,

to anyone who knows

the people inside.

I have had secret fantasies,

about a house all lit up,

with me inside

and you sitting

in your favorite chair,

so inviting.

On Love

One year

I wanted to surprise you,

slip inside your house,

wake up under your tree.

I am like a child now,

believing in magic.

If we were children together,

surely we would be best friends.

No other toy box could lure us away.

We did have special moments

when we were enhanced

to child-like behavior.

You were the present

to the life I knew that year.

The bow you placed around my heart

fit well and kept me whole.

Sometime

On Love

on the eve of Christmas

I may cry,

as one would

while indulging in

forbidden fruits

of what could have been.

Yet even still

I know

I have lived

better.

I have lived.

I have loved

on a night

in deep December

filled with laughter

and hope

for the next

New Year.

Ventured Expressions

To safe-keep a love

holding guard

against growth and time,

is to keep safe a life piece.

We have the power to choose.

Let it go by

or mold it to fit the pattern

that we're used to.

Sometimes, i

f we have our glasses on

we recognize a precious slice,

and we want to return

to live it again,

better because of course

by now we know

better.

On Love

If we venture to be bold we go back.

If luck has it's way

we stay

long enough

to know

better.

I have sought answers and

have reached many conclusions

on many subjects,

yet

never

came to an answer for

why

I had gone that time,

that one time

when I should have stayed.

I had a longing to return

On Love

to that slice of my life

when

I was bold enough

to venture,

fearlessly.

Now,

I may not be fearless, but,

Now,

I would be bold

beyond the venture,

Now

I would safe-keep my love

out loud.

Acceptance

I am torn between each piece of myself.

This moment my heart calls.

I want you.

This moment I am a young girl again.

What I know,

what I don't want to know,

is that I am not a young girl anymore.

Not like before, even though

some things are still the same.

Still, I can never have you.

Still I know the difference

between men like you,

who can only offer

a lifetime of heartbreak,

and men who offer

an eternity of love.

On Love

I suppose

every now and then,

like now,

I need to let myself wonder

backward

far enough

to see that young girl.

To see her

before

she knows better.

To see

how far she has to go.

To welcome the comfort

of knowing

better.

To see

I am no longer torn.

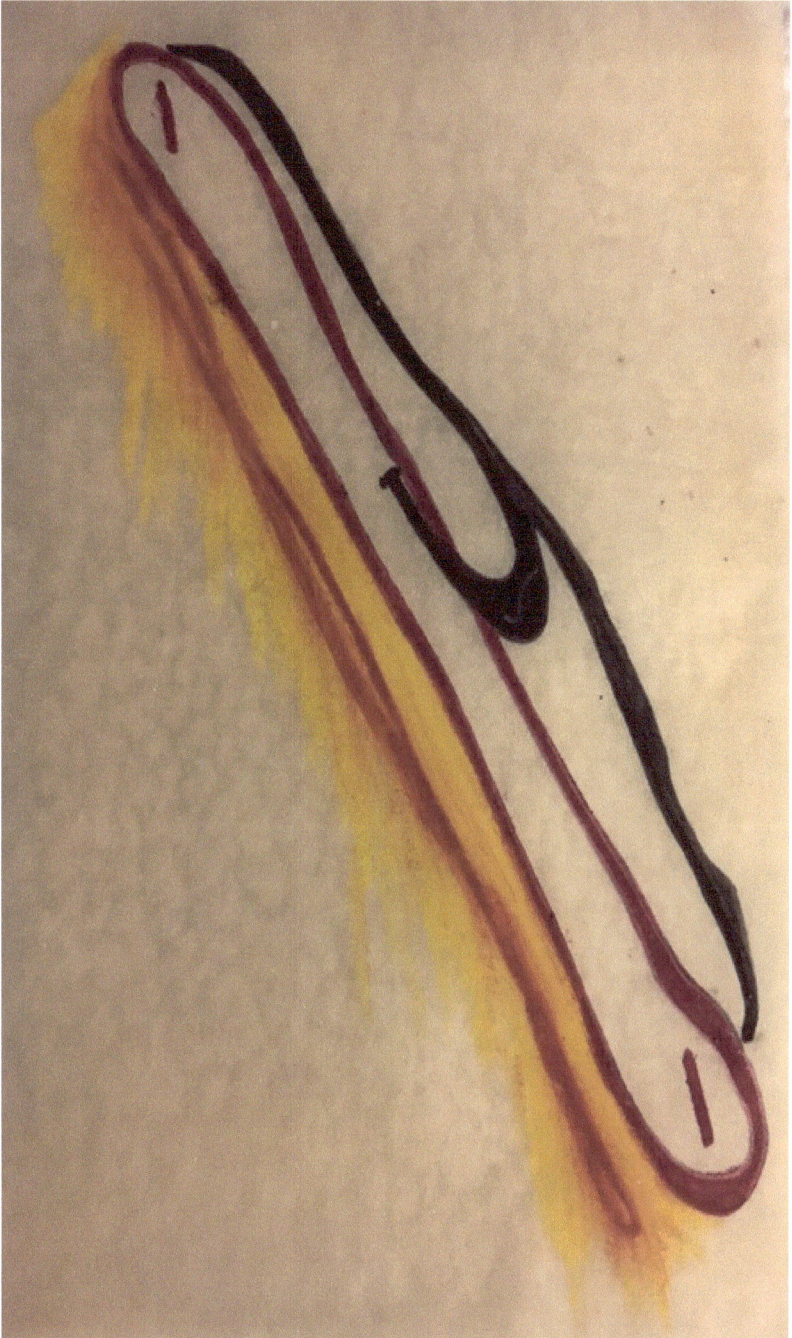

Binding Tie

You, it seems,

are still writing chapters

in my life, on my mind.

Even though I should dislike you

and sometimes do,

I admit that it was you who gave me

new life when I was drifting,

from somewhere, to nowhere.

I only wish

we could somehow,

someday, soon

stop fighting over

the one thing we did right.

So Glad

I am

so happy to have known you.

I am

So happy to be going.

I see

a change is drawing nearer,

Ready-time makes everything

seem clearer

somehow.

So when I go

I may look back

just long enough

to know

there will be no glimpse

of you,

anywhere.

On Love

I shouldn't care

though

I know I will.

Yet I will be

so glad to say

goodbye

for good

this time,

I promise.

So glad to say

goodbye.

You Told Me Once

You told me once

that I should let go

and let my feelings show.

If I did,

I would embrace you

with full abandon.

Then

I would want to stay.

I am not sure

I can handle

your assurance

that it would be okay

or worse

your surprised expression.

As if

that was not what you meant

On Love

or

it was not what you where thinking

or

it was not what you wanted.

If it did not matter

I would embrace you

then turn

and walk away.

I Knew

From the beginning

I knew

that I should have known

better than to try for you.

I knew you were in another league,

with those men who danced until dawn

with all the pretty people.

I knew

that any attempt I made

would seem stupid

and clumsy, yet

there was still something

so exciting

about the possibility

of success.

Something,

On Love

so alluring,

I knew

I could not resist.

I knew

that if I did not try

for you

the regrets waiting for me

would be worse than any despair

I would realize if I failed.

So I made a move

bold and sure

as if I did it all the time.

I knew

at the very next moment

I was mistaken.

I knew

I could not undo

On Love

the damage.

I knew

there would be

no second chances.

I knew

I made the wrong choice.

I knew

I had moved too quickly.

I knew

I would awake

with a haunting recollection

of my err.

I knew

I lost you

before

I ever had you.

The Beginning Of The End

I remember

that precise moment

when everything changed

between us.

I felt a deep hurting sadness

in the core of my being

at that precise moment

because I knew

nothing would ever be the same

between us.

It was in the first light of dawn

when I lay awake

and had a chilling realization

that I was totally alone

even though

there you were

On Love

laying right beside me

with not more

than three or four inches

between us.

I tried to push

the feeling back

but it was too late.

Everything that was left unsaid,

who was right

and who was wrong

no longer mattered

because

It was the beginning

of the end

between us.

On Love

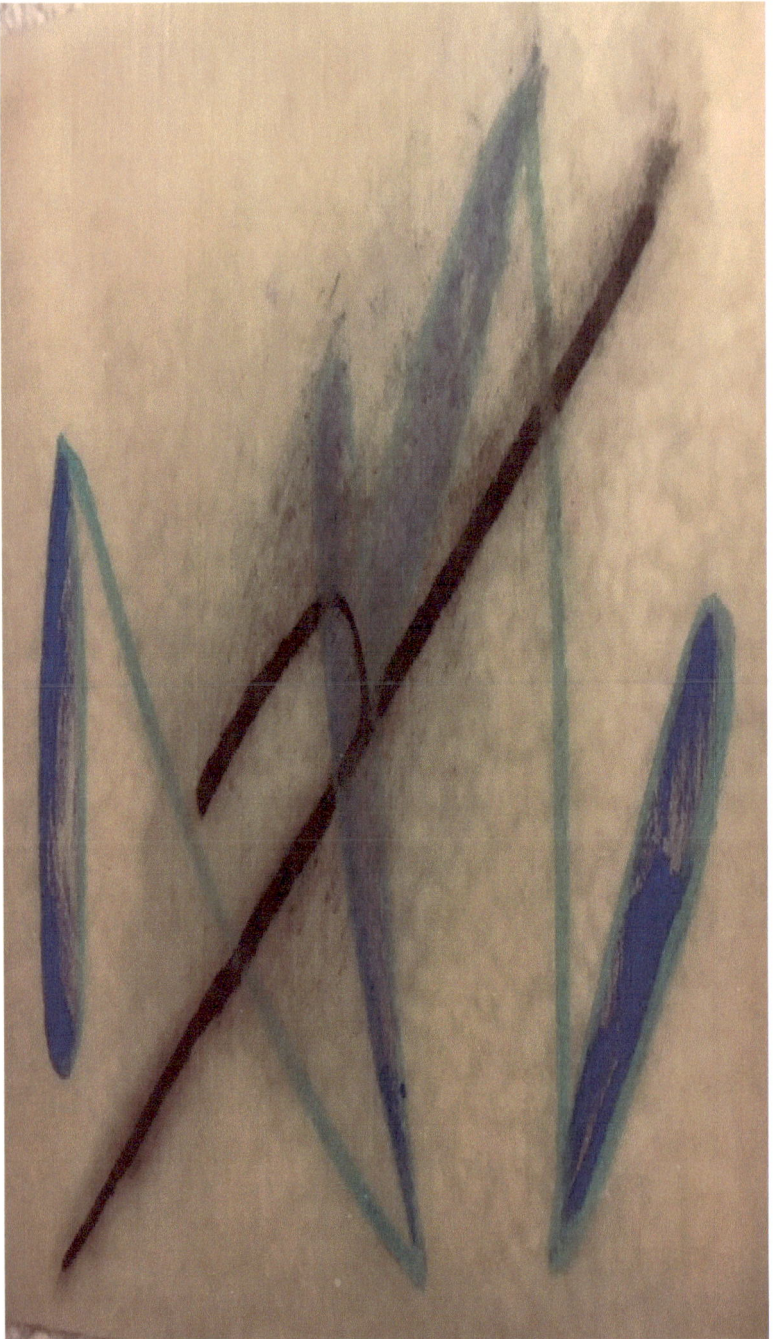

74

The First Dance

When I dance

I lift up

weightless and free

for a brief and happy moment

engaged in movement,

captive by music,

lost in time

still.

Yet

I know

the euphoria

is fleeting and certain

to vanish too soon.

This revelation

bursts the bubble

and now,

On Love

there is no going back,

like to a dream

that ended too soon.

At this precise moment

I see you

standing there

watching

and waiting

for just the right moment

to step in

and join

the dance.

I am uplifted

again

but this time

I am engaged

in the excitement

On Love

of possibilities,

but mostly

I am already captive

by you.

The Last Time

You may not know

that I can feel

your wanting

as you lie here

beside me.

I can hear

the sound of a nearly silent sigh

as your exhaling breath

leaves your heavy laden chest.

I sense that you want to try,

but you know

all too well

that you were the one

who pulled away

maybe too soon

On Love

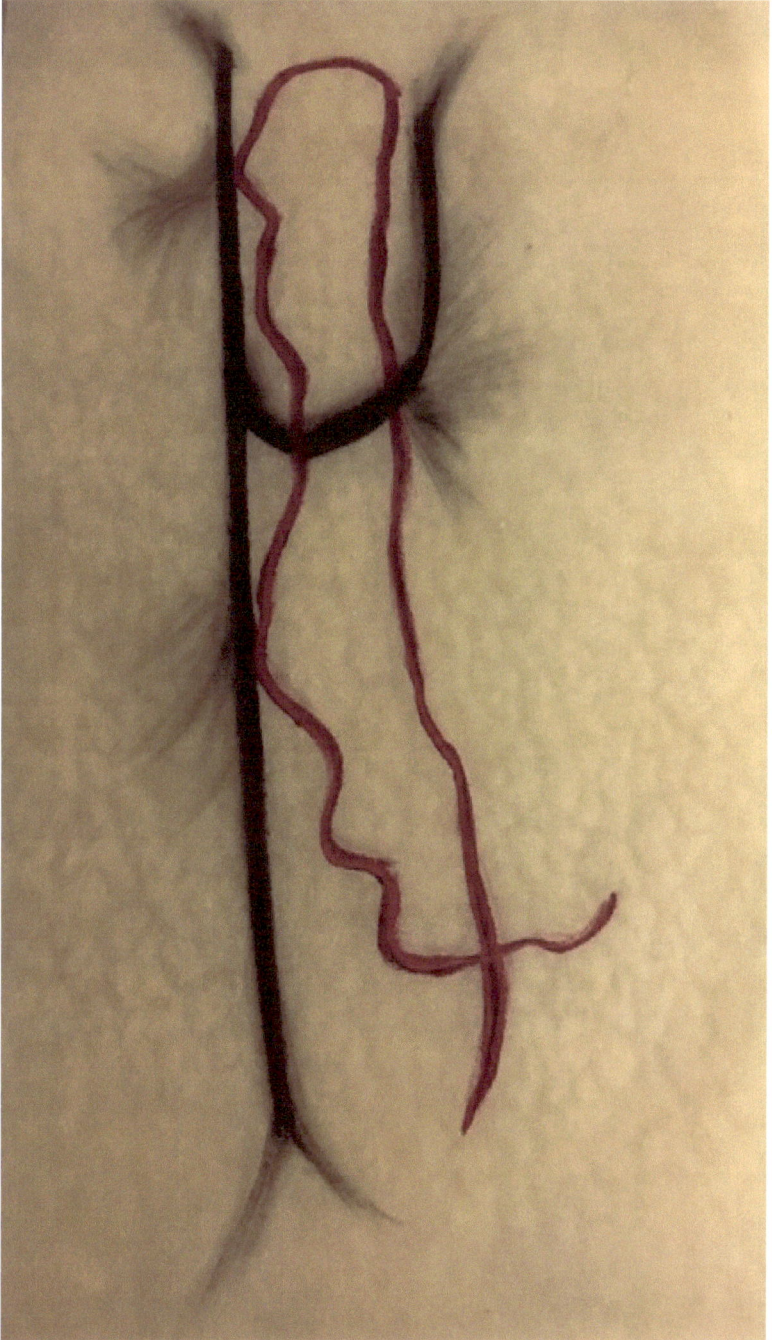

On Love

for me

maybe too late

for you,

but now, right now,

at this moment,

this bittersweet

moment,

I know

that this

is the last time.

I cannot see you

like this.

I cannot see

you

any longer,

you know.

Overnight

A cool ocean mist

sprays your face

just as dawn

is breaking through

a morning sky

painted pastel colors.

A display of beauty

reserved

for early morning risers

or lovers

who spent the night

like we did,

walking side by side,

sometimes holding hands,

or interlocking arms

On Love

like some couples will

when they are most comfortable

in the company

of each other.

Throughout the dark of night

the words flowed well.

Our thoughts

began to entwine with

our souls,

like spiraling vines

spreading and leafy,

with each new breath

we took

of sweet sea air.

As we strolled slowly along,

the cooling sand softly mashing

under each step,

I could feel the power

of the breaking surf,

and the safety in sharing secrets.

Our faces illuminated

only by moonlight filtered

through feathered clouds

moving slowly

across the August sky.

As dawn approaches

we grow quiet.

I am content,

yet not certain

that you feel the same.

I want to say something

but

suddenly the words do not come.

I want to go back to the darkness

but

its cloaked spell is broken.

The seagulls are awake now,

spying for their breakfast.

They run and turn as one

squawking at each other

in sync with the increasing volume

of early daylight's world.

The breeze picks up and

the air is rushing by

cooler now,

as if caused by the awakening movements

of living creatures

while rising

to greet this new day.

I feel a slight chill

and while I close my jacket

On Love

I shift my body slightly

and fix my gaze

your way,

to better see

the expression

on your face

as you stare out

at the ocean,

a remarkably calm backdrop

for my rising anticipation.

As if reading my thoughts,

you turn to me

and smile.

Just like that

it begins.

Take Me

Take me,

here,

let me take you

on a journey

anywhere.

We are seeds

captured in the wind

floating along the moments

that we share,

sometimes stolen,

always shadowed

by a sleepy hue

of uncertainty.

Love's Rugged Road

Stay on love's rugged road

though the path may not be forward.

Circles, so commonplace

yet not anticipated

may be welcomed later

when lessons learned

are forgotten

or misread by the heart.

The time delay

on the merry-go-round

may bring a promise of fortune

or maybe just another day,

without a burnt out bridge

or the death

On Love

of an emotional stage

that is denial.

Stark naked

bears the sorry truth of errs

and humiliation strengthens

one's determination

to continue

trekking along

love's rugged road.

Our Thoughts

I have heard

that maybe

our thoughts travel forever.

If that is true

do you suppose

they are connected somehow?

If they are

could my thoughts

intercept yours at times?

If they can

was that the first time

I met you?

If it was

and if our thoughts are moving

On Love

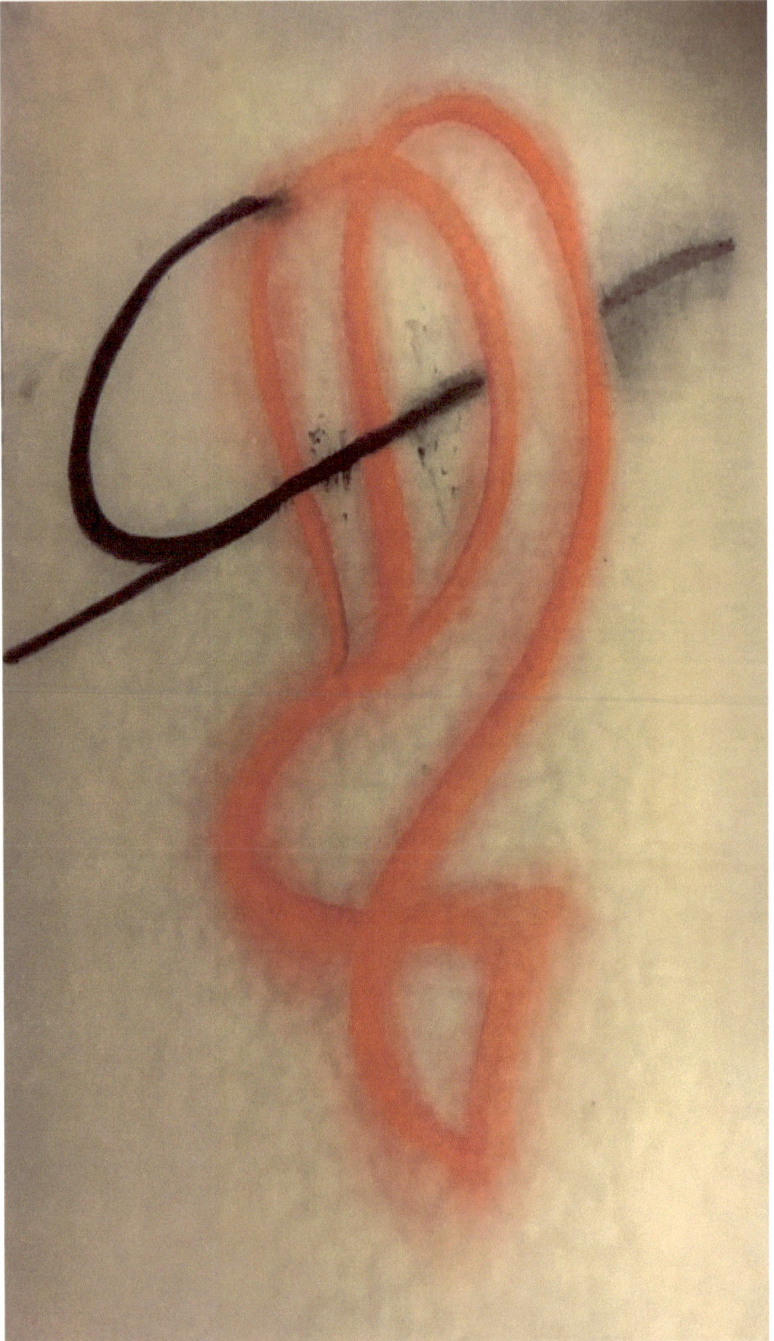

90

in opposite directions

will there come a day

when they will cross again

and we will say goodbye?

I have heard

when we stop the world

we can be our thoughts

and travel

for all eternity.

ABOUT THE AUTHOR

Carol Melber lives and writes on the Central Coast of California where she is inspired by her family and friends every day.